Original title:
A Meaningful Life (Or Just a Good Nap?)

Copyright © 2025 Creative Arts Management OÜ
All rights reserved.

Author: Samuel Kensington
ISBN HARDBACK: 978-1-80566-131-3
ISBN PAPERBACK: 978-1-80566-426-0

Tales of the Unseen

In the land of snoozes, dreams take flight,
Where napping heroes bask in light.
They conquer pillows, soft and wide,
With feathery shields, they take their stride.

Chasing clouds with sleepy eyes,
They dodge alarm clocks, oh what a surprise!
Each yawn a battle cry, loud and bold,
In their cozy forts, so brave and cold.

Snoring symphonies fill the air,
As drowsy knights don their slumber wear.
They twirl in sheets, a tangled mess,
In the quest for naps, they feel no stress.

So when you ponder life's grand schemes,
Remember this tale of cozy dreams.
For laughter waits in hibernation,
In the sock drawer of procrastination.

Evaporating Insecurities

I stand on the scale, what do I see?
A number that laughs right back at me.
I'd chase my dreams, but they're on a shelf,
Reclining and napping — oh, such a stealth!

Whispers of a Restless Soul

My ambitions are shrunk to a tiny size,
Like socks in the dryer, oh what a surprise!
With thoughts racing fast, like kids in a race,
I've mastered the art of just finding my place.

The Poetry of Pause

Brewing my coffee, I ponder and sip,
While carefully plotting my next little trip.
Should I conquer the world or binge on some shows?
The options are endless, oh where do they go?

Cascading Clouds of Calm

Floating in dreams like a leaf on a stream,
Bewitched by the thought of a pillow and cream.
While life's little worries just waltz out the door,
I giggle and nap — who could ask for more?

The Simplicity of Beneath the Surface

In a nap room, dreams do swirl,
Pillows fluff, and thoughts unfurl.
With each heavenly snooze, I rise,
But the snacks by my side are the best prize.

The clock ticks slow, the world fades away,
In this embrace, I choose to stay.
No chores to do, no plans to keep,
Just heavenly sighs and blissful sleep.

Still Waters Run Deep

Beneath the calm of lazy days,
Life floats by in whimsical ways.
With a wink at the sun's bright beams,
I'll trade the world for pointless dreams.

The fish may think they swim in thought,
But I'm the king, without a plot.
Swimming circles in my head,
Where every stress is safely fed.

Meditation on a Cloud

I float upon a cotton ball,
Imagining I'm ten feet tall.
With all the fluff that dreams can bring,
I ponder life and also cling.

Raindrops joke about their fall,
While I enjoy this light bouquet.
Each patter's laugh a gentle tease,
Take me away, oh sweet breeze.

The Dance of Light and Shade

I chase the sun, oh what a game,
Dancing shadows, never the same.
With every tilt, laughter's flare,
In this merry waltz, I have not a care.

As day gives way to the twilight glow,
I pirouette through thoughts that flow.
In the rhythm of what a snooze could give,
Life's tangled mess feels good to relive.

Seeking Serenity in Quiet Corners

In a nook by the fridge, I find my peace,
Where sandwiches linger until my release.
The sound of a crinkle, the rustle of chips,
I ponder the meaning of life through these sips.

Each nap on the couch feels like pure delight,
While the clock ticks away, I'm ignoring the light.
As dust bunnies dance in the soft, gentle breeze,
I chuckle at shadows that tease and that please.

In Pursuit of the Gentle Pause

Coffee's my fuel for the morning race,
But a snooze on the cushions brings plenty of grace.
I chase after moments, but they slip right by,
Like trying to grab clouds in a clear, sunny sky.

The grass calls my name for a quick little lay,
While my mind wanders off to what's for buffet.
Maybe this nap is my ticket to bliss,
Where dreaming of snacks is the ultimate kiss.

Moments That Matter

I'm busy not working, just practicing Zen,
Reclined in my chair, I'll be back... but when?
Socks on the floor are my only real strife,
Am I living it up, or just napping life?

The cat takes a spot on my lap with a sigh,
As I contemplate dinner and give it a try.
Should I stir up some chaos or stay where I'm at?
With dreams of a feast, I expect a big chat.

Waking Dreams

I float on my pillow, a cloud of pure fluff,
Counting my blessings and snacks, yes, that's enough.
The world outside buzzes with a frantic beat,
But here in my fortress, all's cozy and sweet.

I glance at the clock and it's lost track of time,
Is this waking life? Or just napping sublime?
If laughter and napping both bring me delight,
I'll choose to embrace both by day and by night.

Moments Between Heartbeats

In the rush, I spill my tea,
While the cat gives me the eye.
Life's a dance, absurd and free,
Who knew naps could pass me by?

Chasing dreams that slip away,
Yet here I am, just eating snacks.
The clock ticks on, oh what a play,
As I plot my next long nap attacks.

Breathing in the Present

I take a breath, then eat a chip,
Savoring crumbs like fine cuisine.
In my chair, I start to slip,
Does this count as a routine?

Moments pass, I can't complain,
Where's the rush that's driving me?
Falling into joy or pain,
I'd rather nap beneath a tree.

The Paradox of Time

Time's a prankster, can't you see?
One minute's work, the next it's play.
Yet here I sit, just sipping tea,
　Wondering how I lost the day.

Between the tick and tock of clocks,
I ponder life, then hit the snooze.
Existential thoughts like paradox,
But really? I just need some snooze.

Lullabies of the Soul

Whispers soft as cotton candy,
Melodies of dreams and naps.
Life's too wild, oh so dandy,
I'd rather hug my cozy wraps.

Count the sheep, or just the flaws,
Life's a circus, full of fun.
Yet here I bask without a pause,
A nap's my art, my masterpiece won!

Unraveled Threads of Thought

In the tangle of dreams I lie,
Where my socks vanish, oh me, oh my.
Should I chase ambitions or catch some Zs?
A nap sounds grand, like a breeze through trees.

Philosophers ponder, they swim in the deep,
While I float on pillows, drifting to sleep.
What's the secret to a life that's bright?
Maybe it's just to snore day and night!

Should I knit wisdom with needles of fate?
Or lounge on the couch, recreate the great?
Each thought is a thread, getting lost in the weave,
But napping's delightful, oh, I do believe!

In the end, it's a game of nap or to cheer,
Laughing at choices that pull us near.
For in the silliness, joy takes its flight,
Living's amusing, especially at night!

Echoes of Ephemerality

Dancing with dreams on a lazy afternoon,
Chasing the sun and avoiding the moon.
I ponder my purpose, then doze and drool,
Stirring in slumber, feeling quite cool.

Each giggle of laughter like petals in air,
As I think of the world as I lounge with no care.
A fleeting thought like a butterfly's tease,
Maybe this nap could just bring me some peace.

The clock ticks softly, my mind takes a ride,
Some might seek fortunes, but I just abide.
Sleep songs whisper a never-ending tale,
While plans and the universe set sail.

When life is a buffet of choices and fun,
So why not indulge in a not-so-hard run?
The jester inside me knows what to do:
Flip the pillows and welcome the snooze!

Serendipity in the Subtle

Wandering through life, like a cloud blown by air,
Searching for joy, or maybe a chair.
A slice of good fortune, a wink from the fate,
But I trip on my laces and laugh like a mate.

The universe giggles as I bob and weave,
Clutch a slice of pizza, oh what a reprieve!
Should I seize the day or just loaf and snore?
Life's quirks give me giggles, who could ask for more?

In this silly ballet, of mishaps and plays,
I'll nap off the blunders in the sun's warm rays.
With dreams that tickle, and laughter that blends,
This absurd little journey keeps me on trend.

So here's to the moments we chuckle and sway,
Finding pure joy in the mess of the day.
Sleep is the canvas where memories dance,
Life's best is found in a whimsical chance!

Wavelengths of Serenity

Floating on clouds in my cozy abode,
Turning life's chaos into a broad road.
Do I need an agenda, or just a good snooze?
Each nap a rhythm, which path should I choose?

We tumble through life with a playful sight,
As the clock hands tease, say it's time to bite.
Is the afternoon lull a detour ignored?
Or a magical moment where dreams are restored?

With chuckled reflections and giggles so spry,
Life's quirks are the fabric, oh my, oh my!
Should I dance through the chaos or sip lemonade?
Or simply embrace this blissful charade?

Serenity hums in the drowsy delight,
As I journey through whimsy, igniting the night.
Here's to the naps, the laughter well-earned,
For in missed connections, true joy is discerned!

Treading Water in a Sea of Thought

I drift on waves of endless dreams,
Thoughts racing like fast-flowing streams.
Should I splurge on coffee or take a nap?
Caught in currents of life's endless map.

With each splash, I find a new plan,
To conquer the world or just catch a tan.
My mind's a boat that's hard to steer,
Navigating chaos with a chuckle and cheer.

Sunbeams and Daydreams

Sunshine falls on my tousled head,
I ponder if I should get out of bed.
Chasing rays or counting sheep,
In slumber's embrace, where I dive deep.

Tickling thoughts like stray little bugs,
Do I seek wisdom or just cozy hugs?
With giggles and grins, I plot my quest,
In this cartoon that I call my rest.

The Pulse of the Present

In the now, I wiggle and sway,
Avoiding the rush of the fray.
Should I jump into the frills of today?
Or lounge about and let time play?

With snacks in hand, I take a pause,
Loving my life, with its quirks and flaws.
The seconds tick, but I won't be frazzled,
I'll dance in the moment, feeling dazzled.

Navigating Life's Labyrinth

In twisting paths, I blaze my trail,
With socks mismatched, I hardly feel frail.
Do I take the left or the right?
Decisions are tricky, but they feel just right.

Every corner holds a new delight,
Like finding chocolate late at night.
So here I meander with laughter and cheer,
Enjoying the maze, with no end near.

Slumber's Gentle Embrace

In cozy sheets, I nestle tight,
Dreaming of snacks and endless night.
The world spins round, but here I lay,
Counting sheep until it's day.

The blanket whispers soft and low,
To wake or nap? Oh, where'd time go?
A pillow fort, a fortress grand,
With toy soldiers at my command.

Alarm clocks ring, a blaring sound,
But sleepyheads are glory-bound.
Just five more minutes, or maybe ten,
I'll conquer dreams, then wake again.

So let the day scoff and frown,
While I explore my sleepy town.
With giggles and yawns, I'll take a ride,
In slumber's arms, I shall abide.

Reflections in the Quiet

In the stillness of a snoozing room,
Thoughts drift like petals, one by one, in bloom.
I ponder life, and ice cream too,
With stars that giggle and wink at you.

Should I wake and work, or stay in bed?
A battle wages inside my head.
But oh, the charms of peaceful dozing,
With plushies around and pillows frozing.

Reflecting on naps, my favorite sport,
A winning game without a court.
With sleepy grins and dreams galore,
I think I'll just snooze a little more.

So here's to quiet and gentle sway,
To finding joy in the nap we play.
Let life unfold, a fun parade,
While joyfully guessing the time I've laid.

Hues of Happiness

In shades of slumber, I paint the day,
With brush strokes soft, in a dreamy sway.
A splash of laughter, a dash of cheese,
Colors of joyous, mirthful ease.

Pajamas bright like summer sun,
Every pillow fight is a battle won.
With giggles echoing through the air,
Creating joy without a care.

Each napping hour, a vibrant hue,
A kaleidoscope of dreams so true.
A world of fun in every rest,
Where whimsy swirls, and hearts feel blessed.

So let me linger in sleepy bliss,
Paint my dreams with a sunny kiss.
A canvas alive, with every nap,
A splendid masterpiece, without a trap.

Finding Warmth in the Chill

When winter winds blow with icy bite,
I bundle up, much to my delight.
With a woolly hat and two mismatched socks,
I bring the warmth that cuddles and rocks.

Under blankets piled high, I snuggle tight,
As if the world outside has taken flight.
Hot cocoa in hand—life's little thrill,
In frosty quiet, I pause and chill.

A distant snowman winks and sways,
While I enjoy my lazy days.
Fluffy clouds drift, a gentle dance,
In this chilly realm, I take my chance.

Finding joy in every chilly breath,
Life's real fun is when I rest.
So here I'll stay, in a warm embrace,
With frosty smiles, in my cozy space.

The Beauty of Quietude

In a world so loud and spry,
Sometimes silence gives a sigh.
A cozy nook, a gentle chair,
Whispers of dreams float in the air.

The cat sprawls wide, without a care,
Claiming the sun, like it's a share.
A moment's peace, oh what a find,
With droopy eyes, we leave the grind.

Echoes of a Serene Heart

Tick-tock goes the clock, it's true,
But who can hear it? Not this crew!
Sprawled on beds with snacks in reach,
The best of lessons life can teach.

The world's a stage, but I have seen,
The finest act is quite serene.
With giggles soft and dreaming deep,
I'll waltz through naps, my heart will leap.

Blissful Respite

Oh, the joy of snoozing late,
Dreaming big while life can wait.
My pillow's soft, my blanket wide,
In the land of nod, I take a ride.

To-do lists wait; they have their place,
Yet here I find a smiling face.
The world can turn with or without,
While I just nap—there's no doubt!

The Journey Within

Close your eyes and take a trip,
To candy lands with every sip.
Where fairy tales and snacks collide,
And sleepyheads are bona fide.

Floating clouds of fluff and cream,
Chasing after every dream.
Forget the rush, the fuss, the grind,
In sleepy bliss, pure joy you'll find.

The Weight of Unspoken Words

In silence, thoughts begin to pile,
A mountain of words, each one a trial.
I think of chatting while I snooze,
But then I dream of dancing shoes.

The cat takes over my cozy chair,
I think it knows it's only fair.
Each time I shout 'you're the best!',
The echo just gives me a rest.

Pillow talk with shadows near,
They giggle softly, never clear.
My dreams just roll their eyes and sigh,
I wish they'd help me fly high.

In wakeful hours, I plot and plan,
But napping sounds like a good man's scam.
With every yawn, my plans grow meek,
And suddenly, sleep seems totally chic.

Cradled by the Evening Light

As dusk wraps up the day's old fuss,
I lay down, thinking, 'what's the rush?'
The sun dips low, an artist's stroke,
While I consider sleeping, then I poke.

The stars come out, they wink and tease,
While my eyelids drop with utmost ease.
I ponder life's great, big wide show,
But oh, how I love my pillow, you know?

Dreams blend with giggles of the night,
While I snore softly, feeling just right.
Cuddled by the moon's bright glare,
I hear my dreams laugh, 'How's the air?'

If waking's the price for thoughts so grand,
Then let me sleep—just as I planned.
Each moment lost could blink away,
Who cares when snuggles come to play?

Paths Woven in Whispered Wishes

In cafes, whispers swirl like smoke,
Imagining roads where laughter spoke.
I pick a slice of cake instead,
And dream of places I've never fed.

Among the chats and cups of tea,
I ponder where on earth I'd be.
But reach for snacks does sound more fun,
And they don't judge till day is done.

As wishes echo in my brain,
I try to shape them into gain.
Yet here I sit, no maps in hand,
Just cookie crumbs on which I stand.

If adventures lie in sleepless schemes,
Then let me drift in chocolate dreams.
For paths entwined in silly grins,
Will surely lie where laughter begins.

Fleeting Hours of Bliss

Tick-tock goes the clock with glee,
While I'm plopped down, carefree as can be.
A fleeting hour of blissful doze,
With whipped cream dreams and chocolate prose.

As time escapes, a wink and smile,
I stretch out luxuriously for a while.
But when my nap begins to fade,
I wake up puzzled, but unafraid.

The world outside is bright and loud,
Yet I still dwell beneath my cloud.
Where dreams collide with yawns and grins,
I giggle softly at my own whims.

So let the hustle bustle pass me by,
While I enjoy this nap, oh my!
A life of joy, or just a rest?
Either way, I'm feeling blessed.

Whispers of Dawn's Embrace

Woke up with a great big yawn,
Is the day a challenge or just a brawn?
Coffee calls like a siren's song,
Oh dear, where did my dreams go wrong?

Birds are chirping, I hear them sing,
But all I want is a comfy fling.
Why rush when I can snooze a while?
Can my bed give the world a smile?

The sun is up, it's warming me,
But my pillow is pure luxury.
Do I wander or do I lay?
Maybe I'll roll over and stay!

So here I float on this cotton cloud,
Napping hero, oh so proud.
Adventures wait beyond this door,
But first, I'll snooze just a bit more!

The Art of Serene Surrender

Let me drift in this cozy nook,
Who needs plans? Just read a book.
Naps are bliss, like a gentle breeze,
Why make choices? I'm aiming to please!

I'll trade the world for some sweet dreams,
Life's a puzzle or so it seems.
But right now, I'm a sloth in style,
Tired of thinking, let's rest for a while.

The clock ticks on but I won't care,
For this soft bed's beyond compare.
Forget the lists of "must-do" things,
Here in my nap, true freedom sings.

Awake with a laugh, it's time to rise,
But didn't I have a compromise?
Maybe tomorrow I'll chase the sun,
But for now, this snooze is just too fun!

Daydreams Beneath the Stars

Laying back, the moons all shine,
Wondering if my pasta's fine.
Starry nights with dreams anew,
Can they cook, or just watch too?

Thoughts of grandeur, fame and wealth,
Yet all I crave is a snack and stealth.
What's a galaxy without some fries?
I'll conquer the world with sleepy sighs!

Twinkling stars ask what I'll be,
I mumble 'bout napping peacefully.
So what if I've yet to write a tome?
In my dreams, the universe is home.

Eyes shut tight to this night-bound lore,
My dreams take flight—oh, what a score!
Tomorrow's troubles can wait and wait,
For tonight, I'll simply celebrate!

Chasing Shadows of Purpose

Wandered off in search of goals,
But tripped over my own shoes and rolls.
Purpose dances just out of reach,
Never mind, let's head to the beach!

Granola bars and dreamy pies,
They whisper softly, "No goodbyes."
Sandcastles rise with a perfect plan,
I'm more a napper than a busy man!

The waves crash loud, but I can't tell,
If life's a gamble or just a shell.
Who needs fate when I have this bliss?
Dreaming away in my sandy abyss.

So chase your shadows, do what's right,
I'll chase my pillow till the light.
For in the end, it's not the grind,
But the sweet naps that unwind the mind!

Between the Pages of Existence

Between the sheets of daily grind,
We seek a treasure, young or blind.
Sometimes a couch, a cozy spot,
Can turn the mundane into a lot.

We chase the hours with weary feet,
Yet snoozing seems the grandest feat.
With dreams of tacos, naps divine,
Who needs great quests? Just pass the time.

To ponder deep or simply snore,
What's life for, if not to explore?
But never trust a timer's ring,
The snooze button is a wondrous thing.

In search of wisdom, we all quest,
But isn't dozing quite the best?
With pillows soft and blankets warm,
Reality fades, we feel no harm.

Reverie and Reality

I lay on clouds of softest fleece,
And dream of snacks, oh sweet release.
Waking's tough, but dreams are grand,
I'd trade my day for a milkshake stand.

The clock ticks loud, it gives a sigh,
Yet here I drift in the sky.
With ice cream cones and sunny rays,
Why rush when I can snooze all day?

Reality calls with a mundane hum,
But let me sip on my daydreams, yum!
I'll hit my goals — maybe next June,
For now, just one more snooze, and I'll get my tune.

With coffee cold and plans undone,
I hear the world, but it's less fun.
So I'll recline and let life pass,
Dreaming sweetly on my grassy grass.

The Dance of Time

Tick-tock, the hands do sway,
I question time in a funny way.
Should I work hard or take a plunge,
Into the realm where snoozes lunge?

The clock's a joker, what a tease,
I'll move to dance if you please.
With each tick, I twirl and spin,
When all that matters is just to grin.

So step back, life, do your best,
I'll nap through this amusing quest.
With dreams so wild, who needs a plan?
The dance of time is just a scam.

Give me moments filled with slumber,
In those quiet hours, I'll hear thunder.
A laugh, a joke, it's all a show,
For when I wake, I'll surely glow.

Moments that Matter

Amid the chaos, there's a dream,
A slumber party, or so it seems.
With snacks on hand and laughter loud,
What matters most is feeling proud.

The world is big, the tasks are grand,
But sitting still, I find my stand.
With cozy vibes and naps that last,
I'll catch a break from life's wild blast.

So join the fun, let's laugh and play,
And squeeze the joy from every day.
In each giggle and snooze we find,
The moments treasured, sweetly kind.

So raise a toast to silly things,
And all the laughter that joy brings.
For in a life that's loved, you see,
Naps and chuckles matter, just like me.

Unraveled Threads of Ambition

In pursuit of dreams, I chase my tail,
With coffee in hand, I often derail.
Climbing the ladder, but wait, what's that?
Is it a squirrel or just my hat?

Plans laid out like laundry on the floor,
Spinning in circles, I'm left wanting more.
I wrinkle my brows, I ponder and scheme,
Then trip on my shoelaces, wake from the dream.

In the midst of chaos, I sit back and grin,
Life's a funny circus, let the show begin.
With each twist and turn, I'm caught by surprise,
And realize ambition's just wearing a disguise.

So I'll take my nap, let the world rush by,
With visions of grandeur, and snacks piled high.
For in honest laughter lies the true aim,
As I snuggle up tight, I'll play the game.

Melodies of Unseen Connections

Strumming my thoughts on an out-of-tune guitar,
Hoping for harmony, but I'm left with bizarre.
Notes drift like clouds that lose their way,
In a concert of silence where giggles play.

The world spins around with its upbeat sound,
While I fumble through lyrics, all lost and found.
Looking for rhythm in the dance of the day,
Only to trip on a cat in my way.

Oh, the joy of the chase, the connections we share,
Like trying to sing when you just don't care.
With laughter as music, and whimsy the tone,
In this nonsensical jam, we are never alone.

So I'll keep strumming soft, let the laughter unfold,
Embracing the beauty of chaos untold.
For every slip, and each out-of-tune note,
Is a melody crafted in this funny old boat.

Solitude's Soft Embrace

In my cozy nook, I sit with a sigh,
Wrapped in my blanket, just me and the pie.
Days stretch like taffy, all gooey and sweet,
With a side of distractions, I can't feel my feet.

The clock ticks slowly; it winks with a grin,
Playing a game where nobody wins.
I battle the fridge in a snack-off duel,
While shadows of dishes pile up like a school.

With solitude's hug, I wander and roam,
Through fields of my thoughts, they feel like home.
Imagining epic quests, grand and surreal,
But lost in my nap, that's the real deal.

So next time you're lonely, don't frown or mope,
Embrace the sweet moments, with buttery hope.
For life's a good laugh when you give it a break,
And in solitude's arms, it's you, not the cake.

Reflections in a Still Pond

Peering at stillness, the world mirrors back,
Ripples of laughter, a cute little quack.
Frogs sit in counsel, croaking their tunes,
As ducks join the chorus, beneath the full moons.

I ponder my presence in waters so clear,
"What's life without snacks and a bit of good cheer?"
With reflections of wiggles and silly old faces,
In a dance with the dragonflies, life embraces.

Counting the frogs and their raucous delight,
I muse on the meaning of day into night.
Each splash is a giggle, a poke at the soul,
And the ponds remind me to take things less whole.

So let's bask in the silliness, dance, and unwind,
In the gleam of the water, our worries unbind.
For in each little ripple, a joke does emerge,
Just a splash in this pond, where laughter won't purge.

Shadows in the Sanctuary

In a corner, dust bunnies play,
They dance with shadows, come what may.
Couch cushions hold secrets and dreams,
In this sanctuary, nothing's as it seems.

The cat ponders life on the sill,
Wondering if chasing is worth the thrill.
Each nap is a quest, a journey profound,
Yet all he's found is the warmth of the ground.

Raindrops of Reflection

Puddles mirror thoughts, oh what a delight,
Each drop holds a tale, in the soft twilight.
Umbrellas raised like crowns in a jest,
Who knew the damp could be such a fest?

The clouds chuckle as they let it pour,
Sipping from cupped hands, who could ask for more?
Life's like this raindrop, brief but so sweet,
Dancing through chaos, a humorous beat.

Threads of Uncertainty

In the loom of life, my thread's gone astray,
Knots in my purpose, oh what a display!
Each stitch is a giggle, a twist of the fate,
If I start to unravel, would that be too late?

I'm tangled in dreams, like a dog with a ball,
Chasing reflections, I stumble and sprawl.
Yet laughter's the needle that stitches me tight,
In this fabric of chaos, I'll find some delight.

Enchantment in the Everyday

Coffee spills tales, as steam rises high,
A dance in the mug, a swirl in the sky.
Toasters toast bread with a sizzle and pop,
Each breakfast a magic, I could never stop.

The fridges hum softly, like lullabies sweet,
Whispers of leftovers, a savory treat.
In mundane moments, the sparkles ignite,
Finding joy in the trivial, a whimsical flight.

Lessons from the Stillness

In quiet moments, dreams arise,
Where thoughts can frolic, often wise.
A pillow's hug can spark delight,
To snooze or ponder, day or night.

The cat's great nap is pure success,
Why rush through life? Just find the rest.
With eyes half-closed, try not to blink,
Alertness fades, so just recline and think.

The world spins round, it makes no fuss,
When taking stock, don't miss the bus.
A sprightly jig or cozy chair,
Is napping art? Do I dare to share?

Life's silly truths come clear as day,
Sometimes less is just the way to play.
So grab your blanket, don't delay,
Awakening feels great, or so they say!

Fleeting Fantasies

Dreams dashed on waking, oh what a tease,
A world of wonder, a side of cheese!
Chasing rainbows or napping hard,
Both can make life feel less marred.

Imaginary friends help fill the void,
While far-off lands can leave us overjoyed.
Back to the couch with a wink and a grin,
As fleeting thoughts swirl, let the fun begin!

In dreams, I'm a hero with flair consumed,
But in reality, my socks are just doomed.
The laundry waits with a smirk and a sigh,
But a good nap flies by like a blink of an eye.

So when life beckons us away from play,
Remember the dreams can tickle away.
With laughter and naps, it's silly, it's fun,
Life's quirky moments, oh, how they run!

The Essential Pause

Chasing success or just a great snack,
Find a spot, sit down, and unpack.
With arms stretched wide, let worries drift,
A tiny pause can be the real gift.

The to-do list? It can chill for a while,
A quick jaunt to dreamland, just try to smile.
From thoughts of work to doodling cats,
The mind's a playground for silly chats.

When faced with choices, don't sweat a bit,
Grab a cozy corner and simply sit.
Invent funny tales of faraway lands,
Or nap like a pro, just escape life's demands.

Take time to breathe, let silly reign,
The world keeps spinning, never mundane.
So here's to pauses, short or long,
Each moment's a lyric in your life's song!

Harvesting Joy from the Mundane

In daily chores, where joy can reside,
A sock hunt can fill hearts with pride.
The sound of dishes, a rhythmic tune,
Dancing with mops under the moon.

Gardening's just nature's funny show,
From weeds to blooms, watch happiness grow.
A dust bunny roams like a furry pet,
Each sweep a victory, no need to fret.

Cooking's an art, or a fun little mess,
With spills and giggles, I must confess.
If life gets dull, add sprinkles and glee,
Transform the mundane into a jubilee!

So join the circus of daily tasks,
Smile through moments while life unmask.
What counts is laughter, despite the grind,
Find joy in the funny, and peace in the kind!

The Art of Slowing Down

In a world that rushes by,
I find my pace so slow.
With coffee sips and naps,
I watch the daisies grow.

My to-do list is a joke,
It's scribbled on a napkin.
Why fix the world today,
When I can nap, a champion?

A race against the clock,
Turned into leisurely strolls.
Laughter echoes in my dreams,
As I lose all my roles.

So here's to lazy days,
A wink and restful sigh.
Life's a puzzle shuffled up,
I'll dance while others fly.

Glimmers of Gratitude

Each sprout of green I cherish,
With thanks for all I own.
A mismatched sock's a treasure,
Just reminds me I'm not alone.

Old pizza boxes pile high,
My gourmet home delight.
With every tiny crumb,
I savor each snack at night.

Thankful for the sunshine,
That kisses my sleepy head.
For naps that fill my dreams,
And the warmth of my own bed.

Gratitude's a silly dance,
In pajamas I will prance.
Life's too short for heavy plans,
Let's waltz in our lazy pants.

The Weightlessness of Being

At dusk I float on fluffy clouds,
Like cotton candy spun.
Why tackle life's big questions?
I'd rather have some fun.

Floating on this gentle breeze,
My worries wave goodbye.
I'm wrapped in soft serenity,
Like pillows piled high.

Laughter lifts my spirit light,
A dance of silly glee.
What's the point of heavy thoughts?
Just let it be carefree!

So when the ground feels heavy,
And gravity's no friend,
I'll simply smile and drift away,
Until it's nap time again.

Carpet of Stars

Underneath the night sky bright,
I sprawl out on the grass.
Stars twinkle down like fairy lights,
In the cosmic evening mass.

What's the secret to this life?
It's not about the grind.
It's lying back and dreaming big,
While making naps a find.

A carpet woven from the night,
With giggles and with sighs.
I embrace the chilly breeze,
And count the sleep-filled skies.

With every star that twinkles near,
I wish for peace and cheer.
In slumber's warm, embracing arms,
I find my heart's sincere.

Dreams on the Horizon

Chasing clouds with marshmallow trails,
Jellybeans dancing on moonlit gales.
A bicycle ride through a candy lane,
Giggles echo, joy's uncontained.

Stars wear pajamas, comfy and bright,
Happiness twinkles, a silly sight.
Cereal for dinner, why not embrace?
In a world like this, who needs a race?

Silly ducks in top hats and ties,
Turn the mundane into strange surprise.
Lollipops growing from tree limbs so high,
Who knew dreams could make the heart fly?

Unicorns sip coffee, oh what a fuss,
Every moment's gold, driving the bus.
With laughter as fuel, we journey afar,
In this wonderful realm, we're all a star!

Awakening to Now

Alarm clocks ring, but I hit snooze,
Dreams of pastries, brightly infused.
Pajamas are glorious, the morning's attire,
In a cozy cocoon, I won't soon retire.

Coffee in hand, with a splash of delight,
I sip and I ponder, this feels just right.
The cereal's a-swirling, a crunchy parade,
Why rush to the world when this peace is made?

The cat's on my lap, and so is my muse,
Inventing new dances in all of my shoes.
Every tick of the clock sings a silly tune,
As I twirl through the day, like a dancing balloon.

This moment's a gift, with sunshine so warm,
Embracing the simple is where I transform.
Who cares about later, when now's full of cheer?
Let's stir up some giggles, for laughter is near!

Sand Between My Toes

Strolling the beach, oh what a delight,
Playing with shadows as day turns to night.
With each splash of water, a giggle escapes,
Creating memories like colorful capes.

A sandcastle fortress, under the sun,
Where jellyfish waltz, and sea turtles run.
Seagulls play lifeguard on marshmallow skies,
As ice cream dreams melt, it's quite the surprise.

Flip-flops a-floppin', I dance with the breeze,
While seaweed giggles, tickling my knees.
The tide comes a-calling, it pulls me near,
With each wave that crashes, I harbor no fear.

So let's run wild and splash without care,
In this sandy wonderland, life's a fair share.
Trading worries for laughter, let the good times flow,
In this puddle of joy, my heart starts to glow!

The Weight of Feathered Moments

Floating like clouds on a cottony beam,
Time drips like honey, it feels like a dream.
With marshmallow pillows, I snuggle up tight,
In the land of sweet slumber, everything's right.

Feathers of laughter drift softly around,
Whispers of joy in an upturning sound.
I play hopscotch with shadows, round and around,
Where giggles are currency, flaky and brown.

My eyelids grow heavy, inviting me in,
A world without worries, where chaos can't win.
Each tick of the clock is a feathered embrace,
In the dance of a nap, I spin in sweet grace.

So let's tiptoe through dreams, with whimsy in stride,
In this featherweight moment, my silliness rides.
Wake me for breakfast, but until then,
I'm diving in deep, where sweet dreams never end!

Reveries in the Midday Sun

In the daylight's lazy embrace,
Dream of adventures, yet stay in place.
Soft pillows beckon, oh what a tease,
Why climb tall mountains when I've got these?

The sun smiles down, a golden ray,
While my thoughts wander and lightly sway.
Chasing nothing, just floating along,
Catch a sweet nap, right where I belong.

Clouds drift by, their secrets unfurl,
Whispers of laughter in a sleepy whirl.
With snacks in hand and dreams in tow,
Who said the best things must always glow?

As the day fades into twilight's hue,
I snicker at life—who knew it was true?
Deep slumbers are treasures, bold dreams in flight,
Embrace every wink—the world feels just right!

Silk Threads of Gratitude

Life's tangled web can bring a grin,
Like a laundry day with a cat within.
Thankful for crumbs and sips of my drink,
Every small joy makes me stop and think.

Stitching up memories, bright with cheer,
Baking sweet moments, a cupcake here.
A surprise in the oven, who knows what's next?
Perhaps a delight, or simply perplexed.

With each little tick of the clock, I see,
That laughter and smiles are the threads of glee.
So dance with your socks, embrace the mess,
Life's oddities make the best kind of jest!

So here's to the flubs, the slips, and the falls,
To naps on the couch in our fuzzy-warm shawls.
Let's spin tales of joy in this grand charade,
For laughter we weave is never to fade!

The Harmony of Stillness

In the stillness of midday, I find my groove,
The world slows down, just let it soothe.
Birds keep chirping in a silly song,
As I smirk at the chaos, all day long.

Tick-tock goes the clock, yet I ignore,
A nap seems wiser, let's settle the score.
Whispers of slumber creep softly in,
As I drift away with a mischievous grin.

The sweet scent of snacks floats through the air,
A dance of delight, without a care.
Just me and my blanket, in endless embrace,
In this grand symphony of my own space.

So, let others fret about the ticking time,
I'll be dreaming of cupcakes, sipping on lime.
For what is success, if not a good snooze?
In the harmony of stillness, I simply choose!

Echoes of a Revered Journey

The road ahead is paved with snacks,
Every pit stop's filled with giggles and quacks.
Maps sprawled out, yet I take a bend,
To linger a moment and call it a trend.

Unraveled thoughts, like spaghetti on plates,
Wanderlust dreams? Oh, please—those can wait.
In the echoes of laughter, I splash and I dash,
With naps as companions, life's quite the clash!

Each adventure's filled with whispers and grins,
I'll take silly detours, collect the odd wins.
For what is a journey, if not with delight?
To skip through the chaos, and nap through the night.

With every step shared, the giggles grow loud,
In this strange little life, I feel quite proud.
So raise up a toast to naps and the fun,
In echoes of laughter, we've all surely won!

Navigating the Still Waters

Amidst the calm, I found my chair,
Drifting through thoughts, without a care.
Fishing for meaning in a cup of tea,
Dreams of doing nothing, just me being me.

Swapping my tasks for a bit of shade,
Watching the clouds, my leisure well-paid.
Paddling gently in a sea of bliss,
Wondering why I ever thought I'd miss.

Shallow reflections in a still, blue pond,
Echoing laughter from a life beyond.
Who needs the rush when calm is so sweet?
With a nap on the horizon, we're quite upbeat!

So let the waves come, let the chaos swirl,
I'll sit on my raft, with thoughts that unfurl.
Cheers to the lazy, the happy, the free,
For in still waters, I've found my glee.

Whispers at Dawn

The sun peeks out to tickle the night,
A soft little giggle, what a delight!
Stretching my limbs in a sleepy parade,
Each yawn a reminder that dreams can cascade.

Coffee brews while I ponder the day,
Should I conquer mountains or just drift away?
Birds chirp sweet secrets, 'wake up, it's grand!'
But my pillow's a palace, oh, isn't it planned?

With pancakes flipping, they dance in the pan,
I could rule the world, or just flap with a fan.
Whispers of purpose float on the breeze,
Yet the joy of a snooze is what truly frees!

So I'll sip the sunbeams, a morning delight,
Telling myself it's okay to take flight.
For in this dawn laughter and slumber entwine,
Life's just a chuckle, and naps are divine.

Solitude in the Midst of Noise

With city sounds buzzing like bees in a rush,
I find my own rhythm, a quiet little hush.
Dodging the chatter, I nestle away,
In my nook of calm, where the wild things play.

While others are racing on life's speedy lane,
I'm vibing with goldfish, no method to the gain.
What's the hurry, I ask with delight,
When every laugh and nap feels so incredibly right?

Frogs croak my anthem, the wind sings a tune,
Here in my sanctuary, I'm howling at the moon.
Surrounded by chaos, I'm sippin' my tea,
In this bubble of bliss, I'm just happy to be.

So let the horns honk, let the engines roar,
I'll build my fort of pillows and snore.
Solitude found, and a grin on my face,
In the noise of the world, I've found my own space.

Glimpses of Grace

A stumble, a trip, as I make my way,
Life laughs with me, what a comical play!
Graceful moments sneak in like a thief,
While I'm busy searching, they turn me to leaf.

Finding joy in each misstep I take,
Falling through laughter, no need to forsake.
Life's little quirks make me trip like a clown,
In this cavalcade of quirks, I wear my crown!

Bumping into sunshine, hugging a tree,
Who knew grace could be so earthy and free?
A dance in the kitchen can lead to delight,
When you twirl off the floor, and laugh with your bite.

So I'll chase after giggles, and dance with the breeze,
Collecting these moments like petals from trees.
Each stumble a treasure, a story in space,
In this silly adventure, I've found my own grace.

Sighs Under the Stars

In the dark, I lay and dream,
Of simpler times, and ice cream.
Counting sheep? That's too much work,
I'll just snooze and avoid the jerk.

The cosmos blink, my eyelids fall,
Galaxy whispers, it's such a ball.
Are those my worries floating by?
Nah, just the neighbors' cat in the sky.

What's the meaning of this night?
Could it be snack? Oh, that feels right!
But here I am, trapped on my bed,
In this dream of snacks, I'll be fed.

So let's embrace the stars above,
In my dreams, I find my love.
A meaningful life or just some sleep?
Who needs answers? I'll count the sheep.

The Canvas of a Calm Heart

I sat to paint my life today,
But all I did was snooze away.
The brush was nice, the colors bright,
Yet I just dreamed of pizza's bite.

Amidst the strokes, a giggle broke,
My cat stared hard, the perfect joke.
'Is life an art or nap-time bliss?'
I shrugged and sighed, enjoying this.

A canvas made of dreams so sweet,
The only goal? A cozy seat.
Cotton clouds and coffee sips,
What's more divine than cozy trips?

The masterpiece? A restful heart,
So let this nap be the true art.
Forget the brushes; just recline,
Life's a gallery of catnip wine.

Embracing the Present

I woke up late, the sun in my face,
Pajamas on, a slow-motion race.
Should I worry? Or perhaps I'll eat,
Chillin' on couch, that sounds quite neat.

The world spins fast, but I'm right here,
Flipping through channels, nothing to fear.
In my fortress of cushions, I scheme and plot,
What's for lunch? Oh, there's the spot!

An hour rolls by, I'm still in my zone,
Yet somehow, I feel less alone.
With snacks galore and laughter's sound,
The present's a joy; I've truly found.

I embrace the now, let tomorrow wait,
Tomorrow's snooze button can be my fate.
So here I lounge; that's all I need,
In this joyful present, I'll plant my seed.

The Grace of Simple Things

A morning brewed with coffee's scent,
Snuggling in my blanket tent.
The world outside can wait in line,
I'll just sip and feel divine.

A toasted bagel, butter smear,
Who needs fancy? Joy is near.
Life's not glam or glitzy show,
It's in the crumbs and woozy flow.

Chasing dreams? I'll take a break,
The couch is calling; for goodness sake!
With laughter bubbling, and heart at ease,
The joy in nap is pure heart's tease.

So here's to life's simplest chase,
A warm cup and a happy place.
When heavy thoughts start to sting,
Remember — grace is in simple things.

The Fabric of Contentment

In cozy corners, I do reside,
With snacks and naps, my joy can't hide.
The world rushes on, but here I stay,
In my fuzzy socks, I'm ruled by play.

A puzzle piece, I'm not too fit,
Just stitching laughter, bit by bit.
My happy quilt has colors bright,
Each thread a giggle, pure delight.

The cat is king on my throne of cheer,
As I sip my tea, no stress is near.
Why chase the clock? It blinks, it hops,
When life's sweet fabric has no stops.

So let them hustle, let them race,
I've got my nap, my happy place.
In every snooze, I find my gold,
In silly dreams, my heart unfolds.

Paths of Peace

On winding paths where laughter flows,
I take the detours, where the wind blows.
With each step light, I twirl and dance,
To everyday songs, I take my chance.

I met a snail, who shared his tales,
Of slow adventures, and how he sails.
With shells like dreams, he glows and grins,
Reminding me that joy begins.

The flowers giggle in sunlit beams,
They whisper secrets, share my dreams.
I stroll through gardens of blissful fun,
Each step a giggle, my heart on the run.

With every twist, the path unwinds,
In playful journeys, happiness finds.
No rush, no worries, just pure delight,
In the calm of nature, everything's right.

A Symphony of Stillness

In quiet corners, I take my seat,
With snacks and silence, life feels sweet.
The stillness hums a gentle tune,
My chair rocks softly under the moon.

The clock ticks slow, it sips its tea,
While I plot naps, merrily free.
This orchestra plays a lullaby,
As dreams waltz in and worries fly.

The couch is waiting, a plush embrace,
Each little snooze, a joyful chase.
With every yawn, the world drifts away,
In my symphony, it's here I stay.

Dancing with shadows, giggles abound,
In this sweet stillness, joy is found.
No need for a fast-paced ballet,
In peaceful slumber, I love to play.

Mosaic of Moments

In bits of laughter, life is made,
A dance of colors, where worries fade.
Each moment shiny, a joyful spark,
I collect them like leaves in the park.

Sandcastles rise, then wash away,
But memories linger, bright as day.
With splashes of fun and gentle sighs,
In this mosaic, my spirit flies.

The cookie crumbles, the ice cream drips,
Just sprinkle some joy on these little trips.
From sunny shades to starlit nights,
Each memory painted in vibrant lights.

So gather the fragments, stitch them tight,
In this tapestry, everything's right.
With each sweet moment, our hearts align,
In this joyful mosaic, life is divine.

Threads of Purpose

I woke up at dawn, so bright,
Dreamt of glory and lofty height.
But breakfast called, oh what a fight,
Pajamas still on, it felt just right.

Life's grand goals, I left behind,
In favor of snacks and a lazy grind.
Chasing big dreams seems poorly timed,
When donuts are left, the best you'll find.

To climb mountains or snooze away,
Each choice I make, comes with a play.
Should I leap or just delay?
Couch adventures lead me astray.

So here I lounge, no spark or flair,
With every show, I catch fresh air.
Am I a sage, or simply unaware?
Life's a jest, I just don't care.

In Search of Whispers

In shadows deep, I lay to rest,
Dreams of travel, I feel so blessed.
But all my plans were put to test,
When the couch calls, I feel the best.

The world awaits, or so they say,
While I sip coffee and drift away.
Adventure's nice, but I'm okay,
With reruns playing all the day.

With whispers soft, they beckon me,
Yet still, I wonder, what could be?
In cozy realms where dreams fly free,
I find my bliss; it's fine, you see.

So hold your goals or let them drift,
Life's just short; enjoy the gift.
Find peace in chaos, give yourself a lift,
And let good laughter be your shift.

The Art of Stillness

In quiet rooms, I hold the key,
To all the wonders, just wait and see.
No grand designs, just a funky spree,
As I lounge here with my favorite tea.

The world spins fast, with tasks to chase,
But here I am, with time to waste.
Quiet moments bring such grace,
While chasing the bugs upon my lace.

Do I seek fame, or just some fun?
With all these thoughts, I come undone.
For every moment, I've just begun,
The art of stillness, oh it's a pun!

So here I ponder, don't make a sound,
Life's silly whispers, they swirl around.
In frozen time, with snack-y mound,
I find my joy, serenity found.

Chasing Shadows of Contentment

A sunny day, shoes on my feet,
Thoughts of progress, oh what a feat.
But comfy beds are far too sweet,
Thin dreams fade, as I choose the seat.

Chasing dreams, a whimsical spree,
Where's my passion? I cannot see.
In the midst of all this jubilee,
The snooze button is now my decree.

Who needs mountains when couch is near?
Adventure calls—oh dear, oh dear!
Life's great moments disguised in cheer,
With remote in hand, I have no fear.

Contentment found in pillow hugs,
Life's just snuggles, and lazy shrugs.
So hold your plans, I'll meet the bugs,
In this world of warmth and fuzzy rugs.

The Silence Between Heartbeats

In the hush before a snore,
Dreams pounce like cats on the floor.
Fleeting thoughts twist and twine,
Chasing shadows with a glass of wine.

A nap can cure the daily grind,
Yet what's lost, we seldom find.
Perhaps it's magic, soft and sweet,
Or just our tired, aching feet.

Tick tock goes the lazy clock,
In a hall where thoughts do flock.
Here lies wisdom in repose,
Or maybe just a snagged up nose.

So close your eyes, let worries fade,
In this grand parade of the fade.
Giggles sprinkle through the bliss,
In naps, we find our inner miss.

Lullabies in the Laughter

Chasing giggles through the air,
As pillows whisper 'take a dare.'
Cracks in laughter soften the day,
Like rubber ducks in a ballet.

Snoozing under bright blue skies,
Daydreams wink with playful sighs.
Even the sun takes a cozy nap,
In the silly folds of a fluffy cap.

Crumbs of joy fall from our sleeves,
As we weave tales no one believes.
A nap or two tossed in with care,
Leaves us tangled in a love affair.

So let the tickles stir the breeze,
While nap time rustles in the trees.
Find your quiet, sweet reprieve,
In the laughter we choose to weave.

Framework of a Daydream

Building castles in the clouds,
With giggles loud and thoughts so loud.
Lay down bricks of joy and cheer,
With nothing but a cozy beer.

Frames of slow and silly schemes,
Painted boldly with our dreams.
Nap time strikes a funny pose,
As we snooze, the world just goes.

Architects of our soft delight,
Romping 'round till we see the light.
But what's that? A sound we hear?
Just a cat with a wayward leer.

So let the dreams construct their tale,
While our minds set sail without fail.
In slumber's grip, the magic grows,
A canvas where the laughter flows.

Embers of Tranquility

Embers glow in lazy light,
As we drift on pillows slight.
Life's hustle takes a quirky leap,
In the funny folds of a dreamy sleep.

Bouncing thoughts like bags of sighs,
Fill the air with sleepy lies.
Maybe naps are golden cheats,
Or just warm hugs that nature greets.

While clocks conspire to tick and talk,
Explorers lost on a teddy's walk.
The world spins on in silly grace,
While we nestle in our cozy place.

Let's tiptoe to where daydreams flow,
Where time stands still and laughter's slow.
In the ember's glow, we play our parts,
In this grand theater of joyful hearts.

Beneath the Surface of Time

Tick-tock, the clock plays games,
Chasing dreams like wild flames.
Should I seize the day with glee,
Or snooze away, a nap's decree?

Time slips by, a sneaky thief,
But snoozing brings such sweet relief.
Pondering life while I recline,
Do I seek purpose or just a good sign?

My bed's a realm of endless dreams,
Much better than life's boring schemes.
Jobs and bills can wait awhile,
While I nap and dream in style.

Awake to chaos—it's a mess!
But so is life, I must confess.
So maybe napping isn't a crime,
Just the art of bending time.

The Colors of Calm

Sunshine bursts in shades of cheer,
While I lounge without a fear.
The world outside can spin and swirl,
But in my dreams, I dance and twirl.

Life's a canvas, splash it bright,
With vibrant naps that feel just right.
Brush strokes of chill, I wield with glee,
In my cozy corner, wild and free.

Patterns blend, a cozy hue,
As I ponder what to do.
Should I craft a grand design,
Or enjoy this moment—purely divine?

Tomorrow's waiting, let it call,
But here I sit, enjoying it all.
In colors bold, I paint my fate,
Napping dreams, I contemplate!

Dreamscapes and Realities

A nap invites, a tranquil zone,
Where wild adventures can be grown.
Do I journey to distant lands,
Or just rest—with snacks in hand?

Funny thoughts and silly schemes,
Bubble up in sleepy dreams.
Reality's loud, it likes to shout,
But napping's what it's really about!

Coffee waits, but I hit snooze,
Diving deep in dreamfish blues.
A party with unicorns, oh my,
While the real world can't pass me by.

Awake, I find my socks don't match,
But laughter's the prize I always snatch.
In dreamscapes, life's quite absurd,
I'll join the fun—no thoughts deterred!

A Tapestry of Tomorrow

Threads of gold and blues entwined,
Weave a tale that's one of a kind.
Shall I stitch my dreams anew,
Or linger longer, nothing to do?

Sleepy head, now where to go?
Weaving futures, soft and slow.
The loom of life can buzz and clatter,
But naps make everything feel better.

Fabric of days, it twists and turns,
In cozy corners, my spirit yearns.
Shall I labor, focus, and strive,
Or nap and keep my joy alive?

Tomorrow waits with open arms,
But I prefer these little charms.
A tapestry of naps and dreams,
Much sweeter than life's loud screams.

www.ingramcontent.com/pod-product-compliance
Lightning Source LLC
Chambersburg PA
CBHW051635160426
43209CB00004B/659